ROMEO AND JULIET

with Related Readings

TEACHER'S GUIDE

AUTHOR

Chris Ferguson

THE GLOBAL SHAKESPEARE SERIES

I(T)P *International Thomson Publishing*

Albany • Bonn • Boston • Cincinnati • Detroit • London • Madrid • Melbourne • Mexico City
New York • Pacific Grove • Paris • San Francisco • Singapore • Tokyo • Toronto • Washington

I(T)P® International Thomson Publishing
The ITP logo is a trademark under licence

The trademark ITP is used under licence.
Published in 1997 by
International Thomson Limited
1120 Birchmount Road
Scarborough, Ontario
M1K 5G4

ISBN 0-17-606614-4

Cataloguing in Publication Data

Ferguson, Chris (Jeannie Chris)
Romeo and Juliet with related readings. Teacher's guide

(The global Shakespeare series)
Includes bibliographical references.
ISBN 0-17-606614-4

1. Shakespeare, William, 1564–1616. Romeo and Juliet.
I. Shakespeare, William, 1564–1616. The Tragedy of Romeo and Juliet with related readings.
II. Title. III. Series.

PR2831.A1 1997 Suppl. 822.3'3 C97-930744-9

Project Managers: Tara Steele (Canada)
Laurie Wendell (U.S.A.)
Jackie Tidey (Australia)
Production Editor: Sandra Manley
Sr. Composition Analyst: Daryn DeWalt
Cover Design: Liz Harasymczuk
Text Design: Daryn DeWalt
Cover Illustration: IGNITION Design and Communications
Production Coordinator: Brad Horning

Printed and bound in Canada by Mothersill Press

5 MSP 00 99

ABOUT THE GUIDE AUTHOR

Chris Ferguson is the Curriculum Director for the Central Texas Tech Prep Consortium in Temple, Texas. Formerly the Department Head of English at Burnet High School in Burnet, Texas, she has taught English, drama, and speech communications for over 15 years.

Contents

About *The Global Shakespeare Series* Developers

Dom Saliani, Senior Editor of *The Global Shakespeare Series*, is the Curriculum Leader of English at Sir Winston Churchill High School in Calgary, Alberta. He has taught English for over 25 years and has published a number of poetry and literature anthologies.

Chris Ferguson is the Curriculum Director for the Central Texas Tech Prep Consortium in Temple, Texas. Formerly the Department Head of English at Burnet High School in Burnet, Texas, she has taught English, drama, and speech communications for over 15 years.

Dr. Tim Scott is an English teacher at Melbourne Grammar School in Victoria, Australia, where he directs a Shakespeare production every year. He wrote his Ph.D. thesis on Elizabethan drama.

Yuan Lee created the artwork that accompanies the play *Romeo and Juliet* in *The Global Shakespeare Series*. He has a master's degree from the Art School of the National Taiwan Normal University and a master's from the School of Visual Arts in New York. Yuan has taught art at the Henry Street Settlement in Manhattan and has won first prize in the Fine Arts Exhibition of the Republic of China and the Art Exhibition of Taiwan. Yuan is currently working in New York City as a painter and illustrator.

36 Ways to Bring Shakespeare to Life in the Classroom

1. Begin with the student: Commit to a student-centred approach. Shakespeare's work is a vehicle to help students develop a life-long appreciation of the power of language. Focus on the students rather than an in-depth analysis of a classic. Many of the following activities and ideas will help to create a more student-centred environment.

2. Address Why Shakespeare Continues To Be Studied: Challenge students to come up with reasons why we continue to study Shakespeare. This is preferable to telling them why Shakespeare is important or good. Turn the question around so that "Why teach Shakespeare?" becomes "What can Shakespeare teach us?"

3. Teach a Comedy: Many students complete their study of Shakespeare without ever being exposed to a comedy. If a tragedy is on your must-do list, why not follow it up with the study of a comedy? You need not do the play in detail—a film study is often enough.

4. Analyze Dramatic Monologues Together: Before you start a play, choose as many as ten of its dramatic monologues, including the most difficult ones, and reproduce them for the class. Explain to students that the purpose of a dramatic monologue is psychological self-revelation. There is a physical setting and a silent but physically present audience. Have students, in groups or individually, consider the monologues. What is revealed about the speaker's state of mind, motivation, plans, and emotions? Have students create a character sketch of the speaker based on the information in the monologue.

5. Encourage Role Playing: Before dealing with a scene that involves a major conflict, have students role play the situation in a modern context. Discuss the students' role play, leading into the focus of the scene.

6. Go to a Play: There is nothing like a live theatre production of a Shakespeare play. If possible, attend a production as a class.

7. Bring in an Actor: Invite a local actor with an interest in Shakespeare to visit your class. Some actors can give specialized performances designed to introduce Shakespeare to students. Ask your drama teacher for ideas or contacts.

8. Compose Insults: Using the reproducible master on page 43 of this guide, have students compose insults that could be used against characters in the play. Have each student say an insult and ask the class to guess the intended target.

9. Be a Casting Director: Have students cast the play using media celebrities, giving the reasons behind their casting choices.

10. Use the Drama Room: If your school has a drama room/theatre, borrow it for a period. Give students the opportunity to perform a short scene—or even just several lines—from the play. Make the drama teacher your partner and resource.

11. Create a Tableau: Choose a key scene involving several characters. Have students place themselves to show clearly what the relationships, conflicts, and themes are in that particular scene. The other students can be spectators or directors.

12. Perform a Scene in Pantomime: Ask students to perform a scene without words, using only non-verbal sounds and motion to express the meaning. This forces students to concentrate on the action. It also sharpens their awareness of what language can accomplish that sound and action cannot.

13. Perform a Reader's Theatre Script: A Reader's Theatre presentation is essentially an enhanced reading, with selected use of lighting, music, sound effects, costume, makeup, facial expression, and gesture. Have groups of students deal with a scene or act using Reader's Theatre techniques. Each group should have a student director to coordinate the group effort.

14. Use Makeup and Masks: Makeup helps to create character and is an essential component of the special effects required in some scenes. Have students volunteer to be made up in character by classmates. Use facepaint or invite a theatre professional to demonstrate makeup for the stage. Explore the uses of masks as well, since masks frequently were employed in the theatre of Shakespeare's day.

15. Read in Teams: Students love to read in pairs and groups of three. Watch them pick their own parts, vary their voices to accommodate the different roles, and stop to discuss difficult words and passages.

16. Memorize Lines: Memorizing lines doesn't have to be painful. Have students select and memorize lines from the play that they think would be useful in a particular modern situation. In front of the class, students should describe the situation and then recite the relevant lines. Ask students why people might admire someone who is able to quote from Shakespeare accurately and appropriately.

17. Rewrite Verse as Prose: Have students pick scenes and rewrite them into a prose fiction format. They will need to decide on a narrative point of view and a specific genre. A simpler option is to have students translate a speech or a passage of dialogue into everyday language.

18. Study Other Works Based on the Play: To emphasize the continuing relevance of Shakespeare, study another work that was inspired by the play being studied. A wide sampling of such works is included with the plays in *The Global Shakespeare Series.*

19. Write Poems and Short Stories Based on the Play: Give students a chance to write their own works based on the play. For example, students might like to write poetry from the perspective of one of the characters. Parody and other humorous formats are also popular, but encourage experimentation.

20. Create Stage Directions: Creating stage directions that specify facial expression, movement, and tone of voice helps students to understand that interpreting Shakespeare involves imagining the characters as people. Show students a page or so from a modern drama that is rich in stage directions, then have them write stage directions for a brief scene from the play. To facilitate this, reproduce a page from the play and then have students cut and paste the dialogue and their stage directions into a finished script.

21. Create Illustrations: Have students choose ten important quotations from the play, then ask them to create an illustration for each one. They might produce original artwork or use appropriate graphics from magazines. Similarly, students could illustrate key scenes from each act.

22. Compare Different Film Versions of the Play: Show the same scene done by a number of different directors and then have students discuss the intention of each interpretation. What effect did the director attempt to create? Which interpretation works best? Why? Students might warm up for the video comparison by writing their own screenplay for the scene.

23. Arrive at the Meaning of the Work Independently: Allow students to come to their own meaning of the play. Model for them what is involved in a Shakespeare study in the first three acts, then allow them to work through the text themselves.

24. Open Project Formats: Offer students the opportunity to respond to the play in any format they choose. Brainstorm a long list of possibilities. Have them submit a project description and keep a log, recording the problems they face and their attempted solutions. They should present their projects to the class, with each presentation lasting three to ten minutes. Criteria for evaluation should be established when the projects are assigned, and students should do a self-assessment of their work based on these criteria. The self-assessment should include a personal reflection on what they learned about the topic, about themselves as learners, and about their problem-solving abilities.

25. Write Top Ten Lists: Have students compose top ten lists based on important issues within the play, for example: the top ten statements that describe Mark Antony; the top ten reasons why Romeo is friends with Mercutio; or the top ten reasons why Macbeth trusts the Witches.

26. Play the Jeopardy Game: Divide the class into teams. Each team should prepare six categories and batches of questions with which to challenge an opposing team. Questions should not be trivial or difficult. Play the game. Award prizes.

27. Role Play a Daytime Talk Show: Have students work in groups to write and present talk show interviews featuring characters from the play. The rest of the class can be the studio audience, asking questions of or making statements to the guests. Encourage improvisation.

28. Make a Video: Students might create a video version of one or more scenes from the play. They need not stick to the words in the play.

29. Compile a Book of Quotations: Have students compile their own book of quotations, drawing from the play they are studying. The quotations should be organized into themes, concepts, emotions, or other categories of the students' devising.

30. Create a Children's Book: Individually or in pairs, students might write and illustrate a children's book based on the play. The story does not have to be told from the point of view of the protagonists. A comic book version of a scene or even the whole play is another possibility.

31. Produce a Soundtrack: Students who like music could prepare a soundtrack for a scene, act, or the entire play. Some may even want to present original music and lyrics. Ask them to explain their music choices.

32. Write Obituaries or Wedding Announcements: Have students study the style of sample obituaries and wedding announcements. Then have them write an obit or announcement (depending on whether you are studying a tragedy or a comedy) for one of the characters in the play.

33. Identify Ten Difficult Questions: Each play has its own set of difficult questions. Does Hamlet love Ophelia? Who is the protagonist in *Romeo and Juliet*? Is the ghost of Banquo real or just a figment of Macbeth's imagination? Have students come up with ten difficult questions about the play, then discuss possible answers to these questions.

34. Debate the Authorship of the Plays: Controversy continues regarding who wrote the Shakespeare plays. The issue of authorship appeals to students because they like the mystery, they sense possible injustice, and they enjoy the anti-establishment element of the controversy. Provide students with basic information about Shakespeare's life and works, summarizing some of the most contentious authorship issues. Have them conduct further research and choose a topic for debate.

35. Have a Feast: Top off the study of the play with a feast. Students will have to research what people ate during the time period dealt with in the play. Ask students to prepare appropriate dishes. Be wary of any food allergies students may have.

36. Get on the Internet: There are a number of Internet groups that discuss Shakespeare. Have interested students subscribe to SHAKSPER or EVERMORE or Humanities.lit.Shakespeare. They can post questions and receive replies. Through Schoolnet, they can communicate with students all over the world.

Prologue

SETTING THE STAGE

This sonnet presents, in strong concise language, the tragedy of the play. There can be no doubt about how it will end. As the play unfolds, the audience may *want* a different result, but that wish will not be realized.

Romeo and Juliet is an ideal play for young teenagers. Who better can understand the motivations of these characters than those who are adolescents themselves?

BRINGING THE SCENE TO LIFE

Parallel Plays: Select scenes (or the entire script) from *A Midsummer Night's Dream* to study before, during, or after teaching *Romeo and Juliet.* This play offers a different view of "star-crossed lovers" who manage to solve their problems.

RELATED READING

"The Argument from *Romeus and Juliet*" by Arthur Brooke. See page 26 of this guide for ideas about using this poem in the classroom.

REVIEW QUESTIONS

1. What type of poem is this?
2. What events does The Prologue foreshadow for the play?
3. What is the tone of the poem? Give three examples to support your view.

Fair Verona

There is beyond the Alps a town of ancient fame,

Whose bright renown yet shineth clear, Verona men it name;

Built in a happy time, built on a fertile soil,

Maintained by the heavenly fates, and by the townish toil.

The fruitful hills above, the pleasant vales below,

The silver stream with channel deep, that through the town doth flow.

– from *Romeus and Juliet* (1562) by Arthur Brooke, the primary source for Shakespeare's play

Act I Scene I

SETTING THE STAGE

As is common in Shakespearean plays, this scene quickly captures the attention of the audience, while at the same time laying the foundation for the conflict to come.

Sampson and Gregory—Capulet servants, and Abraham—a Montague servant, introduce the audience to the existence of the feud between the Capulets and Montagues. Most of the main characters are also introduced in this scene, together with their relationship to the conflict: Tybalt—a man with a quick temper; Benvolio—an advocate of keeping the peace; the Prince—tired of pointless violence; Ladies Capulet and Montague—anxious to maintain their families' reputations; and Lords Capulet and Montague—both aware of the need for order.

Fighting breaks out between the two factions. After the violence has ended, the Prince decrees the punishment for further disturbances.

Lord and Lady Montague also reveal themselves as caring parents by trying to discover the cause of their son's noticeable unhappiness. Their nephew Benvolio offers to find out for them, and he subsequently discovers that Romeo is suffering from unrequited love for Rosaline.

BRINGING THE SCENE TO LIFE

Modern Connections: Before reading the play, have the students explore the general topic of love. Begin with a modern love poem, for example, *i carry your heart* by e.e. cummings. The unusual layout of cummings' lines in this poem is appealing to students, and the imagery within the poem will parallel concepts within the play.

Getting Physical: As class discussions begin to flesh out the characters in the play, it will help if the students have a mental image of the personalities involved. In groups of three, have the students create a physical shape with their bodies that symbolizes one of the characters in this scene. If you have more groups than characters, have more than one group do the same character.

REVIEW QUESTIONS

1. Why are the servants of Lord Capulet taunting the servants of Lord Montague?
2. Why does Shakespeare not reveal the cause of the original quarrel? Considering the setting of the play, what might the quarrel have been about?
3. What three roles does Benvolio play in this scene? What kind of person does he appear to be? (Hint: line 234)
4. Which Capulet enthusiastically joins the fray? What reason does he give for doing so?
5. What has Prince Escalus decreed will happen if the civil strife does not cease? Why?
6. Why are Romeo's parents worried?
7. Whom does Romeo love?

Act I Scene 2

SETTING THE STAGE

This scene introduces Paris, kinsman to the Prince. Paris is a fine foil to Romeo, Tybalt, and Mercutio; the latter three are driven by their "spleens," whereas Paris is simply a good man looking for a wife.

Lord Capulet is not only a doting father, but also quite accustomed to making decisions for his family. His acceptance of Paris's suit is very close to a formal agreement, although he does qualify it by saying that Juliet must agree to the marriage.

A ball is to take place at the Capulets' home and a servant is dispatched to invite the guests. He is given a paper containing a list of people to be invited. However, he cannot read. Since the illiteracy statistics for the time are estimated to have been 70–90 percent of the population, it would have been common for an illiterate person to seek out someone who could read. As a theatrical device, this character provides the means to ensure that Romeo attends the feast (in order to see Rosaline). Benvolio's encouragement of Romeo to go to the ball uninvited lies in his desire to see that Romeo is cured of "this same Rosaline."

BRINGING THE SCENE TO LIFE

Historical Context: The play *Romeo and Juliet* does not follow the typical marriage customs of the time, neither in the age of the couple, nor in the actual manner a wedding would have taken place. Divide the students into groups and have them research marriage customs typical of the Renaissance. Each group should report these customs to the class. As the study of the play continues, have the class compare what is happening to what would have been the norm, and explain why it deviates from the custom of the time.

Modern Times: As a class, discuss what might take place in your country today. Discuss whether young men still ask permission from their prospective fathers-in-law, and whether a decision would be made in the absence of the bride. Then divide the class into groups and have each group research a different cultural group with regard to that group's current customs.

REVIEW QUESTIONS

1. What does Paris ask of Lord Capulet?
2. What does Romeo notice as he reads the guest list for the servant?
3. What is Benvolio's reason for going to the party?
4. What is Romeo's reason for going to the party?

> *Note of Interest*
>
> Line 14. *Earth ... she* – "All my other children are dead."

Act I Scene 3

SETTING THE STAGE

This scene introduces the talkative Nurse who provides comic relief throughout the play, as clearly illustrated in this scene. Her relationship to Juliet is obviously a very loving and caring one, while Lady Capulet appears to be a step removed from this close relationship.

This scene also sets a foundation for Juliet's inexperience in love. When her mother arrives to announce Paris's interest, the news is intriguing to her, but she feels she is still too young to have any real thoughts of marriage.

BRINGING THE SCENE TO LIFE

Comic Relief: Shakespearean scholars debate whether Shakespeare was inserting comic relief here to ease tension and contrast the intense drama, or if he was simply presenting humorous characters for his audience to enjoy. Ask the students to discuss this idea in small groups, and then have them present their opinions to the class. This project may begin here and continue for a few more scenes before the reports are made. As an extension, have the students debate this issue and then follow the debate with an essay.

REVIEW QUESTIONS

1. What lines illustrate Nurse's relationship to Juliet?
2. What is the purpose of the conversation between Nurse and Lady Capulet?
3. How does Juliet indicate that she has not even considered marriage?

Act I Scene 4

SETTING THE STAGE

Throughout the play, Shakespeare uses more than 160 puns, many of which appear in this scene. However, the scene is not just a series of plays on words—it also foreshadows death. Some scholars claim that Mercutio's "Queen Mab" speech is actually a poem that Shakespeare wrote for another medium and included in this play because it fits nicely. However, there are others who say that this is the axis on which the entire play turns. Whichever view is true, these lines still portray the conjectural quality of humanity's dreams. This speech also gives depth to Mercutio's character: a fun loving teenager, but capable of intense soul searching.

Romeo's last lines in this scene reflect back to The Prologue and the idea of star-crossed lovers. This brings a solemn end to a scene that began in laughter—an element that continues throughout the entire play.

BRINGING THE SCENE TO LIFE

Anticipating: Before the students read this scene, generate curiosity with the activity outlined in the Blackline Master 2 on p. 40. Divide the class into nine groups. Have pairs or groups of students say their line together with emotional impact and a physical gesture. At first, the students may feel a little awkward or embarrassed, but this technique will link them with the lines in the scene, and also add some fun to their study of the play. Discuss as a class possible meanings, but keep the lines out of context to let the students' imaginations have free rein.

Simile Search: Divide the students into teams and have them list similes within the scene. Have the teams take turns, each reading a different simile. Tell the students to cross the simile off their list as it is read aloud. The team that finds the most wins. Once the game is over, ask the students to read the scene for the first time, or again if they have already read it.

REVIEW QUESTIONS

1. What is the purpose of this scene?
2. What instances of good humour are displayed in this scene?
3. Why does Romeo say "And we mean well, in going to this masque, / But 'tis no wit to go"?
4. Write a seven- to ten-sentence definition for dreams, using the words of Romeo and Mercutio.

Act 1, Scene 5

SETTING THE STAGE

Again, this is a scene that begins with light-hearted fun—a clear contrast to the serious end to the previous scene. Capulet welcomes and jests with his guests.

The atmosphere is changed by Tybalt's angry reaction to Romeo's presence. He is quickly and forcefully put into place by Lord Capulet, who realizes that the consequences of violence far outweigh any insult intended. Tybalt, however, vows revenge.

Though Rosaline does not actually appear in this scene, the majority of play productions and movie versions of the play put her in anyway. Regardless, Romeo quickly forgets her as soon as he sees Juliet. This character trait of impetuous behaviour is one of the supports given as the cause of the deaths later on. He continues to act impulsively for the remainder of the play.

Juliet, who is supposed to be looking for Paris, sees Romeo instead. She, too, forgets her previous "love interest." (Like Rosaline, Paris was not written into this scene either, although he also is commonly added in play productions and movies.)

The young couple exchange sweet words of love. As the scene ends, both learn that their love is also their enemy.

BRINGING THE SCENE TO LIFE

Feast and Dance: Provide, or ask the students to find, the steps to a typical Renaissance dance. Divide the students into groups and have them choreograph a dance for the feast. Have them present this dance at the Feast. See the Feast Assignment on page 37 in the Appendix for more details. The students may wish to also make masks, which can be done in or out of class.

Love Images: This scene continues the love theme already introduced. Have the students choose the scene's ten most important lines that express love and arrange them into a ten-line poem. As an extension, ask the students to compose a poem by inserting ten lines from modern songs within those ten lines from Shakespeare. Display these new poems.

REVIEW QUESTIONS

1. What does Tybalt's reaction to Romeo demonstrate about his character? Is this the same Tybalt introduced in Scene 1?
2. Why does Juliet disguise her love for Romeo as a previously learned rhyme?
3. Refer back to The Prologue. What will be the outcome of the love that Romeo and Juliet have professed for each other?

"Love is the strange bewilderment which overtakes one person on account of another person."

– James Thurber (1894 – 1961), American humorist

"Romeo's first appraisal of Juliet's beauty is rich not only in its unforgettable images but also in the subtlety of its wordplay. Hers is a "Beauty too rich for use, for earth too dear." When we recall that *use* means "employment," "interest," and "wear and tear," that *earth* means both "mortal life" and "the grave," that *dear* can be either "cherished" or "costly," ... the line's range of meanings becomes very wide indeed."

– M.M. Mahood, British scholar

A rose will bloom
It then will fade
So does a youth
So does the fairest maid.

– song from Franco Zeffirelli's film *Romeo and Juliet* (1968)

AT THE END OF ACT 1

Reading the First Folio: Have students look at the First Folio page of the play that appears on page 7 of *Romeo and Juliet with Related Readings*. Have them compare this page to pages 14–16 of the text that follows. Have them create a chart to show some of the differences in how the text is presented. They should consider such things as punctuation, spelling, abbreviations, and layout. You may also want to give them the assignment presented on Black Line Master 8 to help them appreciate the editor's role.

Act 2 Prologue

SETTING THE STAGE

Whereas the first prologue established the plot of the entire play, this one summarizes the previous action. It is the second sonnet in the play and was intended to serve the same function as a pantomime, a device often used in Elizabethan drama to foreshadow events in order to keep the audience on track with the plot.

REVIEW QUESTIONS

1. What type of poem is this prologue?
2. What events does this poem reinforce and foreshadow?

Act 2 Scene 1

SETTING THE STAGE

Romeo has evaded his friends and is now standing at the Capulet orchard wall. From this spot, he can hear his friends trying to find him. Again, there is the contrast of the comedic and the dramatic—puns versus allusions to love.

BRINGING THE SCENE TO LIFE

Telephone Conversation: In pairs, have the students script a telephone conversation between Romeo and Mercutio in which Romeo explains why he left without his friends. Ask the pairs to present their written scripts to the class.

Choral Reading: Although it is effective to use single voices, more students will be involved in a group reading. If the students have an opportunity to "touch" the words, they will have more connection to the play. You may wish to assign group roles, or alternately, divide the class into two or three groups and have the group members assign the choral reading parts. Approaching the text in groups is much less intimidating to students.

REVIEW QUESTIONS

1. Is Benvolio's motivation to find Romeo the same as Mercutio's? Why or why not?
2. Why doesn't Romeo wish to be found?

Act 2, Scene 2

SETTING THE STAGE

This scene—the famous "Balcony Scene"—contains the most often-quoted lines from the play. The lines ". . . a rose / By any other name would smell as sweet" are very typical of a Renaissance metaphor for love.

Romeo begins with a monologue in which he declares his love for Juliet. Juliet, unaware that Romeo is standing below her, also professes her love for him. Romeo then reveals himself and the two teenagers decide to ignore family enmity and get married. Juliet will send Nurse to Romeo the next day to get the details of the wedding plans.

BRINGING THE SCENE TO LIFE

Historical Context: In Elizabethan times, the balcony on which Juliet stood may have actually been just a window. If possible, have the students physically create a scene box with a window as the balcony. Ask the students to explain the visual and physical differences between using a window and a balcony. As an extension have the students write a comparison of the use of the two devices, determining which one is most effective in communicating the intent of the lines.

Love Connection: Have the students find a love poem or saying (from sources other than the play). Ask them to illustrate their selection and have a class art exhibition entitled "The Meaning of Love."

RELATED READING

"What the Moon Saw" by Hans Christian Andersen

"Who Cannot Recall" by Philarete Chasles.

See page 27 of this guide for ideas about using these poems in the classroom.

REVIEW QUESTIONS

1. List three objects that Romeo compares to Juliet.
2. List three images that Juliet uses for Romeo.
3. Compare Romeo's reference to a dream in this scene (line 147) to his earlier discussion with Mercutio before the party. Does he apply the same definitions and standards?

Act 2 Scene 3

SETTING THE STAGE

This scene illustrates the close relationship between the Friar and Romeo. Just as Juliet appears to have a closer relationship with Nurse than with her parents, Romeo has a closer relationship with Friar Laurence than with his own parents.

The Friar's opening monologue reveals not only his musing about good and evil, but his awareness of the delicate balance of life. This foreshadows his future actions as he becomes more and more involved in the lives of the two young lovers. The first of these actions is that he agrees to marry them.

BRINGING THE SCENE TO LIFE

Collage: Have the students create a symbol collage of the most important images in the opening speech.

Literary Images: Friar Laurence, in his desperate bid to prevent Romeo from killing himself resorts to using very strong images and metaphors to calm him down. Ask the students to list as many of these images as they can find and discuss as a class how effective they are. Remind the students to use the same devices in their own writing.

REVIEW QUESTIONS

1. What is the Friar's doing as this scene opens?
2. Why does the Friar feel that Romeo's confession is "riddling"?
3. Why does the Friar agree to the plan?

Act 2 Scene 4

SETTING THE STAGE

This scene opens with Mercutio and Benvolio discussing the challenge that Tybalt has sent to Romeo. Romeo enters in an expansive and pleasant mood, a much different person from the depressed young man of the night before. The three of them have a lighthearted, witty conversation.

As Nurse enters, the young men, in their good humour, begin teasing her. Romeo comes to the rescue and informs her that the wedding will be at Friar Laurence's cell that afternoon. Before they part, Nurse mentions the herb rosemary to Romeo (see marginal note 197). This reference is not accidental.

BRINGING THE SCENE TO LIFE

Historical and Modern Context: Have the students research the importance of the herb rosemary and its common uses both during Elizabethan times and today. Then ask them to create a brochure to advertise its uses and benefits.

Realistic Dialogue: Explain to the students that the style in which Shakespeare wrote was appropriate for the time. Although poetic to us, it is not how we would write dialogue for an audience today. Ask the students to write an abbreviated version of this scene, using language that today's audience would expect to hear. You may wish to assign this task to pairs or groups.

REVIEW QUESTIONS

1. Why do Benvolio and Mercutio say Romeo's mood has improved? Cite specific lines.
2. What is Nurse's reaction to Mercutio?
3. What plans do Nurse and Romeo make?

Notes of Interest

Lines 38 – 40. *Now ... berhyme her* – During the Elizabethan period, Petrarch's poems were popular. In his poems, women were idealized and were worshipped from afar for spiritual qualities. Petrarch was a strong example of what it means to love from a distance. Early in life he fell in love with Laura. She, however, married another man and had several children. Petrarch, nonetheless, continued to dedicate numerous poems to Laura.

Lines 40 – 42. *Dido* was a legendary Queen of Carthage who committed suicide when her lover left her. The story of *Cleopatra* and Mark Antony ends with both lovers taking their own lives. *Helen of Troy* was the cause of the costly Trojan War. *Hero* was visited nightly by her lover Leander who swam across the Hellespont to see her, and drowned one night. *Thisbe* and Pyramus were lovers who were separated by walls between their families and met tragic fates similar to Romeo and Juliet.

Act 2 Scene 5

SETTING THE STAGE

Juliet frantically awaits Nurse who has promised to return in half an hour with details about the upcoming wedding. When Nurse finally arrives after three hours she gives no explanation of where she has been. Even then, she coyly delays imparting the information, thus accentuating the fervour of Juliet's emotions.

BRINGING THE SCENE TO LIFE

Mapping Emotions: Brainstorm with the students what colours might be associated with emotions. Ask the students to plot the relationship of Juliet and Nurse in this scene by creating a cluster or a mapping of emotions and words, using appropriate colours for each emotion.

RELATED READING

"Juliet and her nurse" by John Wain. See page 29 of this guide for ideas about using this poem in the classroom.

REVIEW QUESTIONS

1. Why is Juliet so anxious?
2. What lines show Juliet's frustration?
3. What lines illustrate Juliet's anger?
4. What lines show Juliet's happiness?

Act 2 Scene 6

SETTING THE STAGE

This short marriage scene reemphasizes the youth and intense emotions of the couple, as well as the Friar's intention of using this marriage to help end the feud between the two families.

BRINGING THE SCENE TO LIFE

Scene Sketch: Though Elizabethan plays did not have creative backdrops to enhance the drama, modern plays do. Have the students create a sketch of a backdrop for the marriage scene. Explain to the students that colour and geometric design direct the eye of an audience.They must also imagine the emotional response the audience would have to any elements they choose. In addition to the backdrop sketch, ask the students to write a rationale for their design. As an extension have the students choose appropriate music for playing as they present their projects to the class.

REVIEW QUESTIONS

1. Looking at the word imagery presented in this scene, what foundation for love does this couple have?
2. In your opinion, should Friar Laurence have prevented or encouraged this marriage? Give three reasons to support your answer.

Act 3 Scene 1

SETTING THE STAGE

Friar Laurence alluded to the delicate balance of nature and man earlier in the play. In this scene that balance is shattered. Tybalt and Mercutio begin arguing and swords are drawn. Romeo, in trying to stop the fight, causes Mercutio's death.

Once Mercutio dies, Romeo in a fit of rage dispenses his own justice by killing Tybalt. Then, in the line "I am fortune's fool," assesses his own desperate situation and flees the scene.

Benvolio tells the story to the Prince, the Montagues, and the Capulets. The Prince, who has now lost a kinsman, Mercutio, to this family feud, exiles Romeo.

BRINGING THE SCENE TO LIFE

Dueling: Use the following directions to help students learn to choreograph a sword fight. "Swords" that are made out of five or six sheets of rolled newspaper taped at the ends with masking tape are both effective, cheap, and safe, provided that the paper is not rolled too tightly. It is also important to use a whistle or some other attention-getter that will bring everyone to a full stop when necessary. Here are the rules:

1. Only strike on command.
2. Do not touch the body of an opponent.
3. Stop moving and take an at-rest stance when the whistle is blown.

The key to safety is following the rules and paying attention to the instructor. The penalty for not following the rules is non-participation. Since the students will want to participate, getting them to follow the rules is generally not a problem.

Pair the students, making each member of the pair an A or B. Teach the A's, and then the B's the following moves. This should allow them to choreograph a fight scene.

1. Slash from left to right.
2. Slash from right to left.
3. Lunge attack.
4. Overhead slash.

More or different strokes may be added, but too many strokes will take longer to teach.

Be sure to teach the defensive block as well as the offensive blade stroke. The object here is to keep the students from hitting one another, with the exception of the final "killing" blow that will end their fight sequence.

Once the students know the rules and moves, have them choreograph a routine of about ten or twelve strokes.

The students may want to ad lib the duel, but this is not allowed. Explain that the moves must be choreographed and adhered to as carefully as any dance routine. To ensure their compliance, have them write out their routine and tell them you must approve it before they perform. Ask them to practise and then perform their duels for the class.

Comparison: If possible, show clips of this scene from several films to the class. Then have the students compare the attitude of the characters in each version. How does each scene develop a different mood or intensity?

REVIEW QUESTIONS

1. Does weather or temperature have an effect on people, or was the heat a ploy of Shakespeare to lay the foundation of the quarrel? Explain.
2. What lines illustrate Mercutio's disposition toward Tybalt?
3. Describe how Mercutio is wounded, and why Mercutio is critical of Romeo's action.
4. Locate and write out the Prince's original two-line threatened punishment for fighting (lines 86–7, in Act 1, Scene 1). In light of this statement, do you think Romeo's exile is fair? Explain.

Note of Interest

Line 5. In Greek mythology, Phoebus, the god of the sun, rode his fiery chariot across the sky. His son Phaeton tricked his father into allowing him to drive the chariot. Phaeton lost control of the chariot and was killed. Perhaps *runaway* in line 5 refers to the runaway chariot of Phaeton.

"It is one of the puzzles of the play ... that Shakespeare should have chosen to give Mercutio ... a quickness of intelligence, coupled with a quickness of temper expressing itself in trivialities, that produces his own death."

– Derrick R.C. Marsh, British critic

Holden Caulfield from *Catcher in the Rye:*

"I'm not too crazy about Romeo and Juliet.... I mean I felt sorrier when old Mercutio got killed than when Romeo and Juliet did. The thing is, I never liked Romeo too much after Mercutio gets stabbed.... It was Romeo's fault. I mean I liked him best in the play, old Mercutio.... The thing is, it drives me crazy if somebody gets killed — especially somebody very smart and entertaining and all — and it's somebody else's fault. Romeo and Juliet, at least it was their own fault."

– J.D. Salinger (b. 1919), American novelist

Act Three Scene 2

SETTING THE STAGE

As this scene opens, Juliet is speaking her thoughts about love and impatiently waiting for nightfall when she will be with Romeo. Nurse arrives with the terrible news but is unable to give a coherent explanation of what has happened. Juliet first thinks that Romeo is dead, then that both Romeo and Tybalt are dead. When she finally learns the truth she puts herself on the path to her own death. Nurse, against her better judgment, agrees to bring Romeo to her that night.

The wording in this passage is very strong and passionate. It is in this scene that love and death become entwined, as they will be for the rest of the play.

BRINGING THE SCENE TO LIFE

Journal Writing: Have the students create diary entries for Juliet of her feelings. Begin with Juliet's reactions when she first meets Romeo. Bring the diary up to date as of this scene, and as the play goes on have them continue till the last entry she would have made. As an extension, you may wish to ask the students to compile their "diary" into a booklet, complete with small illustrations or symbols.

Personalizing the Text: Have the students illustrate their favourite line in this scene on a large sheet of paper. Ask each student to explain his or her choice. Display the art in the class.

RELATED READING

"On Playing Juliet" by Peggy Ashcroft. See page 28 of this guide for ideas about using this poem in the classroom.

REVIEW QUESTIONS

1. Why is Juliet confused about who is dead?
2. What lines illustrate Juliet's anger when Nurse tries to blame Romeo for what has happened?
3. What does Nurse think Juliet should do now, and what is Juliet's reaction to the suggestion?

Act 3 Scene 3

SETTING THE STAGE

Romeo hastens to the Friar's cell, aware that by killing Tybalt, he has not only broken the Prince's mandate, but more importantly, he has killed the cousin of his new wife.

Typical of some adolescents, Romeo's world is microcosmic. He is unable to see the larger picture and that banishment is not death. His feeling about the word "banishment" is that it is the most horrendous punishment imaginable, and death would actually be preferable. (Juliet's reaction in the previous scene is very similar.) In a fit of despair, he draws his dagger, but is prevented from stabbing himself. The Nurse and the Friar convince Romeo that his banishment to Mantua will be short-lived, as he will soon be joined by Juliet. He calms down as plans are made for him to visit Juliet that night.

BRINGING THE SCENE TO LIFE

Help Hotline: Today, Romeo might look for help from many agencies or hotlines. In Shakespeare's time, his only source of "professional" counselling would have been the Friar. In small groups, have the students discuss solutions to Romeo's situation. You might wish to suggest the students either a) keep the time, setting, and location in mind as they problem-solve; or b) use today's agencies or hotlines as sources where Romeo might obtain help, and what advice might be given. As a class compare and discuss the viability of the solutions.

REVIEW QUESTIONS

1. Using direct quotations, indicate the depth of Romeo's horror of banishment. Why do you think Romeo reacts this way?
2. What reasons does the Friar give for Romeo to count his blessings?
3. What plan does the Friar share with Romeo and Nurse?
4. What does Nurse gives to Romeo from Juliet? Why do you think Juliet sent it?

Act 3 Scene 4

SETTING THE STAGE

Lord Capulet gives his consent for Paris to marry Juliet. His motivation may be simply that he wants to see his daughter safely wedded. Perhaps he is afraid that Tybalt's action in killing Paris's kinsman will make Paris retract his offer of marriage. Or, Capulet may have simply decided that it is time to take real control of his daughter's life. At any rate, he arbitrarily decides the wedding is to take place almost immediately—quickly and quietly, since Juliet is still grieving for her cousin Tybalt.

Shakespeare, in this scene and elsewhere in the play, uses time, or the lack of it, to further his plot. In this case, he wants to prevent an equitable solution to the problem. He does this by not giving the characters enough time to think problems through rationally. Weddings would not normally have been arranged this quickly or this close to the death of a kinsman; however, the proposed marriage does ensure that one rash decision will continue to follow another.

BRINGING THE SCENE TO LIFE

Walk in Lord Capulet's Shoes: Ask the students to write a monologue to add to the play. In this monologue, have Lord Capulet justify the actions that he has just taken. The students may write it in modern English or in Shakespearean style.

REVIEW QUESTIONS

1. When is the wedding to take place?
2. We can understand why Capulet might be agreeable to this hasty marriage, but why do you think Paris is anxious to have the wedding take place so quickly?
3. Explain the significance of this scene in relation to the events that have taken place so far.

Act 3 Scene 5

SETTING THE STAGE

Romeo and Juliet have an emotional parting. Romeo says he would rather die than leave her, but she urges him to go. Their lines here are some of the most poetic of the play.

Lady Capulet enters and informs Juliet that she is to marry Paris. Juliet says deviously that she would rather marry Romeo than Paris. Her mother calls in Lord Capulet whose reaction is swift and decisive: she will marry Paris or he will disown her. She turns to Nurse for help, who advises Juliet to abandon Romeo and marry Paris. Although Juliet appears to comply, her final speech reveals her anger and her intentions to join Romeo or die.

BRINGING THE SCENE TO LIFE

Word Play: Have the students create a comparison chart in which they list the phrases from the scene that have two meanings. Be sure they define the double meaning and explain why it is used.

Cause and Effect: In the previous scene and this one, Shakespeare makes use of cause and effect. Ask the students to work in groups to map out the cause and effect sequences in these two scenes: CAUSE —> EFFECT —> CAUSE —> EFFECT. Suggest that the students make a note in their writing folders to use this structure in their own writing.

Mythology References: Since the majority of people in Shakespeare's time were illiterate, they told and retold stories. In fact, bards, or storytellers, were welcomed everywhere. In all the stories, there would be references to mythological characters who were symbols of concepts and morals. When the names of these figures were mentioned in stories, plays or poetry, the listeners knew these references. Shakespeare used many mythological references in his plays. Using Black Line Master 7, have the students explore some of the mythological references in the play.

REVIEW QUESTIONS

1. To what length is Romeo willing to go to please Juliet?
2. What are Juliet's prophetical words as Romeo leaves?
3. How does Juliet use words in her conversation with her mother to hide her true feelings?
4. How do Juliet's parents react to her refusal to marry Paris? Why do you think they react in this way?

Act 4 Scene 1

SETTING THE STAGE

Paris has gone to see Friar Laurence to arrange for his marriage to Juliet. As he is about to leave, Juliet arrives. Paris's true goodness shows as he gently speaks to Juliet, who responds with words and phrases that have double meanings.

Once Paris leaves, Juliet begs the Friar for a solution to her problem. She even threatens to kills herself, just as Romeo tried to do. Recognizing her desperation, the Friar offers her a very harrowing means of evading the marriage: she will take a potion that will make her appear dead. She will be laid in the family burial vault. When she awakens, she can escape to Mantua with Romeo. The Friar, the key player in all of these plans, promises to get word to Romeo.

BRINGING THE SCENE TO LIFE

Comparing Interpretations: If possible, show the students this scene from the Franco Zefrellini version of the play. Have them analyze how the filming technique emphasizes the text. Replay the scene several times and have the students write their responses in their journal. As an extension, show another version and ask the students to compare and contrast the two.

Personal Response: Ask the students to discuss in groups Juliet's and the Friar's difficulties and behaviour in this scene. You may wish to develop some prompts for the sharing of ideas, such as: At this point, what choices did the two characters have? *Do you think the style of Juliet's responses to Paris are warranted? To what degree is the haste in which everyone is forced to act responsible for the lack of judgment shown? How might Juliet and Friar Laurence have dealt with the situation if they had had more time? Are you in sympathy with them? Why or why not?* After the group discussions, ask the students to have a recorder summarize their responses and nominate a spokesperson to share them with the class.

REVIEW QUESTIONS

1. How does the Friar react to Paris's visit? Why?
2. In what way does Juliet demonstrate her feelings for Paris?
3. What answer does the Friar give to Juliet's request for help? In your own words, list the steps Juliet must follow.

Act 4 Scene 2

SETTING THE STAGE

Lord Capulet, assuming Juliet will bend to his will, sets the wedding preparations into motion. In fact, when Juliet returns, she indeed says she will now marry the County Paris and asks forgiveness from her father. Her father is so pleased that he moves the wedding up to Wednesday instead of Thursday. Shakespeare is again playing with time.

BRINGING THE SCENE TO LIFE

Monologue: Though Shakespeare often used flat characters, Juliet is not one of them. Discuss the differences between flat and rounded characters with the students. Then have the students write a monologue revealing Juliet's true feelings during this scene.

REVIEW QUESTIONS

1. Give examples of how Juliet conceals her true feelings.
2. How does Lord Capulet plan to solve the time problem with regard to the wedding preparations?

Act 4 Scene 3

SETTING THE STAGE

Seeming to comply with what others have planned for her, Juliet asks to be left alone for her final preparations. As she contemplates the possible outcome of taking the potion, all sorts of terrors fill her mind. The wording in the scene is again very powerful and dramatic. Finally, she takes the potion and lays down to sleep.

BRINGING THE SCENE TO LIFE

Terror: Before reading this scene, have the students create a list of things that frighten them. Later, have them compare their list to Juliet's lines. Ask them to write in their journal how their terrors are the same and how they are different from Juliet's.

Tone and Mood: Ask the students to read (or reread) Juliet's monologue at the end of the scene. Ask them to choose the one or two lines that best represent her feelings, and then list all the words and images that contribute to the overall tone of this speech. Suggest they make a note in their writing journal about the importance of establishing and reinforcing the tone and mood they wish to convey to their audience.

REVIEW QUESTIONS

1. What are Juliet's fears about taking the potion? What is her alternate plan if the potion does not work?
2. A well-rounded character is one that is multifacted, like a jewel. What does this scene reveal about Juliet?

Act 4 Scene 4

SETTING THE STAGE

This scene, a contrast to the blackness of the previous one, brings the focus back to the wedding. Lord and Lady Capulet rush about to complete the final touches for the celebration.

BRINGING THE SCENE TO LIFE

Interview Skills: Divide the students into groups of three. Have the groups devise an interview between Lord and Lady Capulet and the society editor for the local newspaper by writing at least ten questions to ask. Tell them to then choose roles (or assign them yourself) and conduct the interview. Assure the students who have been chosen as interviewers that they do not necessarily have to stick to the original questions. It will depend on where the answers lead. Based on the interview, have the group collaborate on writing an article for the society page on the upcoming wedding. As an extension, you may wish to ask them to plan a full page layout for the newspaper, complete with photographs.

Historical Context: During the Renaissance, the actors in a play dressed to fit the part, but without extensive wardrobe changes. What they wore was symbolic of their characters in the role, job, social standing, or archetype. Have the students choose two of the major characters from the play and design a costume for that character to wear throughout the play. To accompany the project, ask them to explain in a few paragraphs why they decided on their particular design. Some research may be called for regarding styles for the time and place.

REVIEW QUESTIONS

1. What is the purpose of this scene?
2. What is Capulet's mood? Give examples to illustrate your answer.

Act 4 Scene 5

SETTING THE STAGE

In this scene Shakespeare again has an actor on stage acting lightheartedly, while the audience knows the tragedy of the scene. At first Nurse gaily goes about waking Juliet until she realizes that Juliet is "dead." Then the scene becomes a "lamentable day."

The Friar arrives and instructs the family to "in her best array bear her to church." He says comforting words to the Capulets and Paris, and leaves to make the final preparations both for the "burial" and to notify Romeo.

The scene ends with another group of characters, this time the wedding musicians, exchanging witticisms.

BRINGING THE SCENE TO LIFE

Role Play: In groups of six, have the students pantomime this scene. Ask them to plan out how they will indicate which person has which part. Give the students adequate time to practise their roles. Some groups might wish to perform their pantomime for the class.

REVIEW QUESTIONS

1. What lines create an almost comic effect, while also lending themselves to high drama?
2. What is the reaction of each of the characters to Juliet's death? Be sure to include the Friar.

Act 5 Scene 1

SETTING THE STAGE

Romeo has a dream of Juliet, finding him dead, revives him with a kiss.

On hearing of Juliet's death, Balthasar, Romeo's servant, rides to Mantua to tell Romeo and then accompanies Romeo back to Verona. On the way, Romeo makes a stop at an apothecary's shop to buy poison.

BRINGING THE SCENE TO LIFE

Letter Writing: Romeo and Juliet would have written to one another as often as possible. Have the students write a letter either Romeo and Juliet would have written up to this point in the play. Tell them to make sure the letters reflect both the characters and the age of the writers.

Writing: Have the students rewrite Romeo's soliloquy by changing the ending Shakespeare wrote.

REVIEW QUESTIONS

1. Describe Romeo's dream about Juliet.
2. What news does Balthasar bring, and what is Romeo's reaction to it?
3. In his speech, what does Romeo tell Juliet?
4. What would we call an apothecary today?

Act 5 Scene 2

SETTING THE STAGE

Friar Laurence learns that his plans have gone awry. The bearer of the letter to Romeo (Friar John) was caught in a quarantine and could not deliver the letter or quickly get a message to Friar Lawrence about the failure of his mission.

Once the Friar learns this, he writes again to Romeo and sets out immediately to attend Juliet's awakening.

BRINGING THE SCENE TO LIFE

Logistics: Shakespeare, like Charles Dickens, used happenstance to forward his plots. Key timing or mistiming was everything. Have the students create a map on which they track the trips for Friar John, Balthasar, and Romeo during scenes 1 and 2 of this act.

Hand Props: At the time of Shakespeare, there were no elaborate scene decorations or props for the actors to use in order to help set the scene. Divide the students into small groups and have them decide what items might have been placed on the stage and what items the two characters would carry (no more than three carried by any one person) in order to communicate a sense of place and time. Once the groups have devised their list, ask them report to the class. Have a discussion on the appropriateness of their choices.

REVIEW QUESTIONS

1. What has Friar John failed to do? Why?
2. What does Friar Laurence feel at this moment?

Act 5 Scene 3

SETTING THE STAGE

Paris is paying his respects at Juliet's tomb when Romeo arrives. Believing Romeo has come to defile her grave, he challenges him. They fight and Paris falls, mortally wounded. Before he dies, he asks Romeo, "open the tomb, lay me with Juliet." which Romeo does. He then accomplishes what he has set out to do—he takes the poison to "set up [his] everlasting rest" with Juliet.

Friar Laurence enters the cemetery and rushes into the tomb, fearing that he is too late. He finds the bodies of Paris and Romeo.

Juliet awakens, sees the Friar, and asks for Romeo. When she realizes he is dead, she refuses to leave the tomb with the Friar when the Watch sounds the alarm. She takes Romeo's dagger and fatally stabs herself.

The Watch sends for the Prince, the Capulets, and the Montagues and detains the Friar, the Page, and Balthasar, Romeo's servant.

The Prince demands "to know how this foul murder comes." The Friar, Balthasar, and the Page sadly fill in the details. Montague informs the group that his wife has died of grief. Montague and the Capulets promise to build a monument to the deaths of their loved ones and the Prince sends them off to reflect on "these sad things." There will be a new "glooming peace" in Verona.

BRINGING THE SCENE TO LIFE

Monument: Have the students individually design a fitting monument for the two lovers. These designs could be put on poster board and displayed in the class.

The Friar's Trial: See marginal note 315. Conduct a class trial of the Friar. Divide the students into groups in the following way: Have some students act as *Friends of the Court* to present arguments supporting the Friar. The arguments should contain quotes and actions from the text to support their ideas. Assign one student to be the Prince, several as representatives of the Montagues, several as representatives of the Capulets, several as advisors to the Prince, and the rest supporters of the Friar. Ask each group to plan their strategies and try to anticipate the strategies of the other groups. Then stage the hearing.

RELATED READING

"Soft—Soft—She Breathes" by David Garrick. See page 30 of this guide for ideas about using this poem in the classroom.

REVIEW QUESTIONS

1. What prompted Paris to visit Juliet's tomb secretly on Thursday night?
2. What command does Romeo give Balthasar? Use quotations from the text to show how strongly Romeo felt about being obeyed.
3. Why would Paris feel Romeo would "do some villainous shame" to Juliet and Tybalt? Under the circumstances is he justified in thinking this? Explain.
4. Why do you think Romeo honours Paris's last request?
5. What does Friar Laurence fear? Why do you suppose he asks Balthasar to accompany him to the vault? Why does Balthasar refuse to go?
6. Why does Friar Laurence leave Juliet in the tomb alone?
7. What has happened to Lady Montague, and why?
8. What purpose is served by having the Page and Watchmen enter the tomb?
9. Why is Friar Laurence able to tell the greatest part of the story? What other characters fill in the gaps?
10. What symbolic action do the Montagues and Capulets agree on to end the feud?

AT THE END OF THE PLAY

Advice Column: Students can readily identify with many of the events in this particular play. Considering the age of the characters, the adolescent love, and the generation gap, most students can step into the world of Romeo and Juliet. Divide the students into groups and ask them to make up an advice newsletter based on the play's events. Tell them to write questions and answers for specific problems encountered by the various characters. You may wish to brainstorm first with the class and assign each group a different topic on which to base their questions and answers.

Putting the Play in Context: In modern theatre, playwrights provide detailed stage directions for the actors and directors. These might be what a particular actor carries, the direction of movement on-stage, and/or diagrams of set designs. These directions provide clues as to the author's intent. During the time of Shakespeare, the scripts used by acting companies had few, if any, stage directions. Generally an *exeunt, alarums,* and such were all the direction given. Throughout the last 400 years, this lack of detailed information has allowed directors and actors free rein with Shakespearean performances. The activities suggested in this guide have given students the option of providing their own interpretations of the presentation and this experience should enable them to see many other possibilities. Show the students the same sections of different movie versions of the play to give them an idea of the variety of presentation styles. (Time restrictions will no doubt prohibit showing films in their entirety.) Have students write an essay in which they describe how this lack of stage direction has kept *Romeo and Juliet* a vibrant and living play.

Idea Starters: You may want to conclude your study of the play with a longer writing assignment. At this point, students may choose a theme, image, or plot element that they would like to investigate further on their own. A number of suggested topics are offered on Black Line Master 9 on page 47 of this guide.

Related Readings

THE ARGUMENT FROM *ROMEUS AND JULIET* a poem by Arthur Brooke

This opening section from the longer poem provides a foundation for understanding Shakespeare's play. Although this poem was translated by Arthur Brooke in 1562, the story is not original to Brooke. He translated it into English from a French translation that had been translated from Italian. The original source is thought to be a Greek romance *Ephesiaca*. The story had been translated and rewritten numerous times. However, it is more than possible that Shakespeare had read only the Brooke version.

SUGGESTED STRATEGIES

Sonnet Search: In groups have the students find out the following information about this type of poem: What are the characteristics of a sonnet? Where did sonnets originate and when? What is the rhyme scheme? What is the usual subject matter? Who are some of the more famous sonnet writers? Ask the students to write a short group report and present it to the class. As an extension, some students might wish to try writing a sonnet.

REVIEW QUESTIONS

1. How long does the married couple meet in secret?
2. What event ends the couple's bliss?
3. In your own words, explain how Juliet avoids a second marriage.

THE AUTHOR

Arthur Brooke (d. 1563) was an English translator who brought the tale of Romeo and Juliet to England.

Notes of Interest

Line 1. twain – two
by sudden – at first

Line 3. shrift – secret; during the time dedicated for confession

Line 4. bower – bedroom

Line 5. three months – In Brooke's poem, Romeus and Juliet meet just before Christmas and they are married within the next few days. They are secretly married for three months before their tragedy begins to unfold.

Line 10. reave – take away

Line 13. bane – poison

LIGHT IMAGES IN *ROMEO AND JULIET* a literary essay by Caroline F.E. Spurgeon

This essay provides a key to some of the imagery of the play through its suggestion that the plot can be directly tied to the interwoven images of light and dark.

SUGGESTED STRATEGIES

Visual Images: Before reading Spurgeon's essay, have the students skim the play text for images of light. Have them create visuals for those images that they find, using construction paper, magazines, and markers. Then ask them to discuss the essay in relation to the visual light images. Are they appropriate? Do they fit with Spurgeon's viewpoint? What would they change?

REVIEW QUESTIONS

1. Explain how Spurgeon connects the compression of time in the play with the light images Shakespeare used.
2. According to Spurgeon, how does Shakespeare use light images in Capulet's words to Paris and in Juliet's lines?
3. What light images are used in relation to Mercutio?
4. What specific images does Spurgeon say Shakespeare took from Brooke's poem? Why does she express surprise that he should have done so?

5. In her final paragraph, the author notes the difference in style between Brooke and Shakespeare. Explain her opinion in your own words.

THE AUTHOR

Caroline F.E. Spurgeon (1869–1942) was the first woman to hold a professorship at an English University (the University of London). She was a specialist in Chaucer and Shakespeare and one of her most popular works is *Shakespeare's Imagery and What It Tells Us,* from which this selection was taken.

WHO CANNOT RECALL
a poem by Philarete Chasles

This short, image-filled poem provides an intense depiction of the atmosphere of the play.

SUGGESTED STRATEGIES

Choral Reading: Have the students do a choral reading of the poem. Afterward, ask them to discuss in groups the poem's impact on them. Ask them what images came to mind as they read?

Vocabulary: Have the students find three words in the poem that are unfamiliar to them. Ask them to define those words and then find words from *Romeo and Juliet* that have the same meaning and intent. Students may choose to illustrate one of the words.

REVIEW QUESTIONS

1. List the sombre images in the poem.
2. What is the basic feeling generated about the play in this poem?
3. How are line breaks used to emphasize words and phrasing?

THE AUTHOR

Philarete Chasles (1793–1873) was a French scholar, essayist, and curator of *Bibliothèque Magazine*.

WHAT THE MOON SAW
a poem by
Hans Christian Andersen

In this poem Hans Christian Andersen has Juliet reflecting on her love for Romeo.

SUGGESTED STRATEGIES

Group Analyzing: Before the students read the poem, divide them into groups. Give each group a portion of the poem to read and analyze. For their analysis suggest they might ask themselves: a) What is the poet describing? b) Is the language appropriate for the subject matter? c) What is the tone? d) What words and phrases provide the tone? e) What personal response did they have to the poem? Allow time for the groups to discuss the poem, and then ask them to present their insights to the class. After the groups have finished their presentations, help the class connect all of the ideas generated to the poem as a whole.

REVIEW QUESTIONS

1. From whose viewpoint is the poem written?
2. Part of this poem is about love and yet it begins with the phrase "Heavy clouds obscured the sky." Why would the poet begin with an image that could be interpreted as bleak?
3. Explain in your own words what the Moon offers the narrator.

THE AUTHOR

Danish writer **Hans Christian Andersen** (1805–1875) is best known for his fairy tales;

however, he was also a novelist and poet. His use of the most ordinary of ideas and concepts in explaining life has given his works an international appeal. Andersen's works have been translated into almost every language in the world.

EXCERPT FROM *WEST SIDE STORY* fiction by Irving Shulman

The movie *West Side Story* was voted best picture of the year at the 1961 American Academy Awards. It is often included in the teaching of Shakespeare's *Romeo and Juliet*. This excerpt describing the first meeting of Tony and Maria is from the novelization of the film.

SUGGESTED STRATEGIES

Personal Response: Have the students discuss in groups what went through their minds as they read the story of Tony and Maria's meeting. How is it similar to reading the same scene in Shakespeare's play *Romeo and Juliet*? How is it different? Alternately, you may wish to ask the students to write a personal response in their journal.

Playing with Words: Have students take words from Romeo and Juliet's meeting in the play, from this *West Side Story* excerpt (which takes place in the late 1950s), and from today's language, and weave those words into a poem based on this scene. Encourage the students to play with the words. They may wish to use the sonnet format for their poem.

REVIEW QUESTIONS

1. How does Tony feel as he enters the room? Why?
2. What keeps Tony from leaving?
3. What is Maria's reaction to Tony?
4. How and why is the magical meeting of the lovers interrupted?
5. What Shakespearean character does Bernardo represent?

THE AUTHOR

Irving Shulman (1913–1995) was a Brooklyn-born novelist and screenwriter. Best known for his work in film, his screenplays include *Rebel Without a Cause*, a teenage tragedy about youth alienation.

ON PLAYING JULIET a recollection by Peggy Ashcroft

This selection clearly illustrates the joy Peggy Ashcroft felt in playing Juliet. She also provides some insight into the difficulties inherent in playing this part successfully.

SUGGESTED STRATEGIES

Personal Impressions: Create a situation in which the students can think about the lines just as Ashcroft did. Ask the students to read lines from Act 3, Scene 2, in groups. Tell the class to make sure each member of their group has an opportunity to read various roles. Then ask the students to respond in their journal to their feelings about the different characters and the words they read aloud.

REVIEW QUESTIONS

1. What does Ashcroft say causes the tragedy within the play?
2. Ashcroft says that although Lord Capulet tries to keep the peace, violence is inevitable. What is her reason for saying this?
3. How many times in total has Peggy Ashcroft played Juliet?
4. According to Ashcroft, what is the most important consideration in playing Juliet?
5. What age range does Ashcroft consider possible for an actor playing the part of Juliet? What do you think would be the best age for the stage part and the movie part? Explain your answers.
6. Explain in your own words two difficulties in playing this part.

THE AUTHOR

Dame **Peggy Ashcroft** (1907–1991) was an internationally acclaimed British actress. She not only dominated the British stage, but was also a winner of an American Academy Award.

JULIET AND HER NURSE
a poem by John Wain

In contrasting the Nurse and Juliet, John Wain poetically defines the essence of both these characters.

SUGGESTED STRATEGIES

Comparison Chart: Have the students create a comparison chart, putting on one side the qualities of Juliet and her Nurse as created in the poem, and on the other side examples from the play that coincide with the qualities from the poem.

Poetry Analysis: Point out to the students that this is a blank verse poem. Discuss with the class what qualities make this a poem and not prose.

REVIEW QUESTIONS

1. Explain in your own words what the nurse's experiences of life are.
2. Which descriptions apply to Juliet? Do you think these descriptions could be applied to any young person in love? Why or why not?
3. What do you think the poet is saying in this poem?

THE AUTHOR

John Wain (1925–) is a British lecturer and professor of English. His writings are dominated by his search for the common elements of knowledge and experience.

Note of Interest

Line 14: *haec, illa* – Latin words both meaning she

LADY CAPULET: A "NEGLECTED" MOTHER
a literary essay by Sarojini Shintri

This essay puts forth possible reasons why Shakespeare portrayed Lady Capulet's character the way he did.

SUGGESTED STRATEGIES

Rewrite: Have the students rewrite and add to Lady Capulet's lines that are quoted in this selection to make her a more rounded character and appear to be more caring of her daughter. Have a class discussion on whether such changes might have a positive or negative impact on the play as a whole if Shakespeare had chosen to flesh out the character in this way.

Discussing Characterization: After reading the essay, discuss as a class whether or not there are other characters in the play that suffer from "neglect" in the same way as Juliet's mother. Then discuss the priorities and constrictions a playwright might have when developing some characters more fully at the expense of "ignoring" others.

REVIEW QUESTIONS

1. What are the reasons Shintri gives for stating that Lady Capulet is a "neglected" character? Do you agree with this rationale?
2. According to Shintri, what are some of the possibilities for Lady Capulet behaving as she does?

THE AUTHOR

Dr. Sarojini Shintri has written about the roles women characters have in Shakespeare's plays. This selection appeared in a research series published by Karnatak University in Dharwad, India.

SOFT—SOFT—SHE BREATHES
a drama excerpt
by David Garrick

About one hundred years after Shakespeare wrote *Romeo and Juliet,* actor and theatre manager David Garrick changed the ending of the play to one that he felt was stronger and had more appeal to the audiences of the time.

SUGGESTED STRATEGIES

Alternate Endings: Authors, playwrights, and screenwriters have been known to change the planned endings to their work. Sometimes two endings of a movie are filmed and preview audiences are asked to vote on their preference, with the most popular choice being used in the final version.

Divide the class into groups and ask each group to choose a book or movie with which most people would be familiar. Have the groups collaborate on writing one or more different endings. Come together as a class to discuss the implications of altering an author's work. Possible topics for discussion: Why do you think the author chose that particular ending? Do people prefer happy or sad endings? Are endings important to the commercial success of a creative work? Is it an insult to an author when other people rewrite part of an original work? Why do moviemakers frequently alter the plots of books upon which films are based?

REVIEW QUESTIONS

1. Create a time line of action for Garrick's rewrite.
2. Find phrases and lines that are the same in both Shakespeare's and Garrick's versions. How much was changed? Do you think this is acceptable?
3. Why did David Garrick change the ending of the play?
4. Do you think Garrick retained the original "flavour" of Shakespeare's wording in his version?

THE AUTHOR

David Garrick (1717–1779), after failing in the wine business, became a successful actor. From acting, he turned to theatrical managing (London's Drury Lane Theatre) and did much to popularize Shakespearean drama. He also wrote for the theatre, mostly in a comedic vein.

WHEREFORE ART THOU PALESTINIAN?
an article by Jeffrey Bartholet

Bartholet describes a courageous joint Arab-Israeli production (June 1994) of a remake of *Romeo and Juliet* set in Jerusalem.

SUGGESTED STRATEGIES

Writing: Have your students do what the producers in Jerusalem did: Ask them to select a conflict and write a short drama about it, based on the premise of *Romeo and Juliet* in which bitter ill-will is changed to love. The students could look to history, current affairs, or their own creativity for their conflict. Have them choose an appropriate setting and era.

REVIEW QUESTIONS

1. Explain the opening two sentences of this piece.
2. What were the producers of the play trying to accomplish?

THE AUTHOR

Jeffrey Bartholet is a journalist with varied interests, especially those that examine cultural diversity. He now works in the Tokyo bureau of *Newsweek Magazine*.

JULIET
a poem by Anna Jameson

The poet tries to explain the deep and inner emotions that the character of Juliet has evoked within her.

SUGGESTED STRATEGIES

Oral Reading: Ask the students to read the poem aloud one line at a time, each line said by a different student. Then have them read the lines one at a time by pairs of students, then one at a time by four students. Then have the whole class read all the lines together at the same time. Once the students have finished reading the poem in this manner, have them discuss the feelings and ideas that come from the poem and how they can be applied to the play text.

Personification: Have the students illustrate and label three examples of personification from the poem on poster board or construction paper. Display the art in the classroom.

REVIEW QUESTIONS

1. How does the author use repetition of patterns and words to emphasize her meaning? Give examples.
2. Looking at the consonants within the poem, how many have hard sounds and how many have soft sounds? Why does the poet use combinations of the same type of sounds?

THE AUTHOR

Anna Brownell Jameson (1794–1860) was a prolific Irish writer who wrote primarily about interesting or notable women. Her works include *Shakespeare's Heroines: Characteristics of Women* and *Memoirs of Female Sovereigns.*

ALBERT, THE PERFECT WAITER
a poem by Bert Almon

This poem is a wonderful character description. It also illustrates the effectiveness of inserting Shakespearean text into other writing.

SUGGESTED STRATEGIES

Quotable Quotes: Have the students choose four quotations from *Romeo and Juliet* and integrate those lines into a description of a person. Tell them to include dialogue as done in the poem. As an extension, the students could illustrate their character.

REVIEW QUESTIONS

1. What manufactured items does the author contrast with natural elements?
2. What idea does the use of the word "kitsch" convey with regard to the last two lines of the first stanza?
2. What personality traits would Albert display in real life based on his description in this poem?
3. Who is the "you" in the poem?

THE AUTHOR

Bert Almon (1943–) is a Texas born poet and professor who now lives in Canada. Author of five collections of poetry, his collection *Calling Texas* (1990) examines his own personal history and the mutability of North American society.

A FAMILY FEUD
a parody by Richard Armour

Not everyone writes seriously about Shakespeare's work. In this parody, Richard Armour provides rare and wonderful "insight" into the plot of *Romeo and Juliet.*

SUGGESTED STRATEGIES

Dramatizing: Have the students stage this version of the play. Be sure to use a narrator to help communicate Armour's concepts.

Debate: Have the class debate the use and effectiveness of parody and satire. You could keep it specific to the play such as "People should (or should not) be allowed to parody Shakespeare" or more general, such as "Parody and satire—does it help or hurt?"

REVIEW QUESTIONS

1. Give three examples of Armour's humour that you find particularly clever (other than puns).
2. Why do you think Armour makes extensive use of footnotes? In your opinion, do these add to or distract from the piece? Explain.
3. Would this version be as funny if you had not read the original play? Why or why not?

THE AUTHOR

Richard Armour (1906–) was born in California. Besides being a noted humorist, Armour has written a number of serious biographical and literary works. He is, however, best known for his humorous treatment of history and the classics.

ROMEO AND JULIET
song lyrics by Mark Knopfler

The lyrics to this song are representative of the many songs about the play.

SUGGESTED STRATEGIES

Listening: Rather than just read the lyrics, it would be effective to obtain a copy of the actual song to play in class. The song can be found on the album *Making Movies* by Dire Straits. Produced by Jimmy Lovine and Mark Knopfler. © 1980 Rondor Music (London). Ask a student to look for a copy if one is not readily available. After the students have listened to the song, ask them to analyze it from the point of view that it is poetry. As an extension, ask the students to create a collage based on the poetic images they find in the song.

Research: Many songwriters write very poetically and their words read as well as they sound when put to music. Ask the class to research songwriters such as Buffy Sainte-Marie and Chris de Burgh, and find examples of their songs. Have a class presentation on the findings of the students. You may wish to ask the students to write a full essay on the topic "Songwriters as Poets."

REVIEW QUESTIONS

1. What scene from the play is the song describing?
2. What message is being conveyed in the song? Is it the same as that of the play? Explain your answer, using quotations from the song.
3. Do you think the song owes any of its approach to the movie *West Side Story*? Why or why not?

THE AUTHOR

Mark Knopfler (1949–) of the rock group Dire Straits is a musician and songwriter. Born in Scotland, he obtained degrees in journalism and English and worked in both these fields before his rock group became famous.

NEW CAREER FOR JULIET
an article by Dora Jane Hamblin

This article reveals not only the world-wide popularity of Juliet, but the dedication of the citizenry of Verona to keeping the romantic legend alive.

SUGGESTED STRATEGIES

Internet Activity: Have the students communicate with other students on the Internet who have an interest in Shakespeare. Ask them to report back to the class their findings on the opinions of others. You may wish to brainstorm a list of possible topics and questions for the students to use as conversation starters.

Symbols: To quote one of the letters in the article, Juliet has become "the symbol of eternal love." There are many other love symbols in cultures throughout the world. Divide the class into groups and have them research these symbols and their specific significance to love. You might assign different cultures or regions of the world for research, or alternately, brainstorm symbols students already know and divide these up for further research on origin and symbolism. (Examples: Valentine's Day, hearts, Cupid, certain flowers, certain foods.)

REVIEW QUESTIONS

1. Why do you think Ettore Solimani and Paola Sella were willing to become unpaid "secretaries for Juliet"?
2. List the Italian words that appear in italics and write the English meaning for each. Find out the origin of the word *italic.*

THE AUTHOR

Dora Jane Hamblin was born in the United States and spent much of her life as a researcher, correspondent, and staff writer for *Life* magazine. She is now a freelance writer living in Italy.

ROMEO AND JULIET
fiction by Karel Čapek

This story is but one of many that have been written about or in response to the theme of Romeo and Juliet. As explained on page 6 in the student text, variations on the story have been traced back as far as the fifth century B.C.E. Shakespeare, apparently, was just one in a long list of writers who became enchanted by the theme. Most people would agree with Sir Oliver's statement that Shakespeare's version is "a thousand times more beautiful" than any other.

SUGGESTED STRATEGIES

Discussion: Have the students discuss in groups whether the play or this short piece is the more "beautiful" story. Come together as a class to exchange ideas. You might wish to list the pros and cons of each. What conclusion can the class come to?

Writing: The selection has another story within its plot. After the students have answered Review Question 4 below, ask them to expand on the information by writing a short story that follows the outline. Post the stories in the class so that they can be shared by all. Alternately, the students could write an entirely new version of Padre Ippolito's story, complete with a different setting.

REVIEW QUESTIONS

1. Give three characteristics of Padre Ippolito. Support your answer with quotations from the story.
2. Why is the priest unaware of who Juliet is?
3. How did Padre Ippolito know Friar Laurence?
4. Write an outline of events as they happened according to Padre Ippolito.
5. Why does Sir Oliver feel the play with its death and tragedy is much more beautiful than the tale of a woman who marries and has eight children?

THE AUTHOR

Karel Čapek (1890–1938) was a Czech journalist, playwright, and writer. He became famous for his works of science fiction and in fact coined the word "robot." The theme of his works was often Utopian.

PURGATORY
a poem by Maxine Kumin

This poem reveals a possible sad state of affairs had the lovers succeeded in escaping to Mantua.

SUGGESTED STRATEGIES

Writing: This poem and the one following, "Romeo and Juliet II," allude to a more realistic ending to the drama. Have the students take these ideas and write yet another version. Explore with the students the possibilities available for short story writing, including the "twist" ending. Remind the students that although unhappiness or sadness may make for more drama, happy or fairy-tale endings have their place in literature also.

REVIEW QUESTIONS

1. What is the tone of this selection?
2. Explain the following in your own words: "cheat the crypt"; "displeasing cockerel"; "posts a purse"; the last line of the poem.

THE AUTHOR

Maxine Kumin (1925–) was born in the United States. Her poetry deals with the search for survival and common elements in everyday lives. She won a Pulitzer Prize for her book of poetry *Up Country* in 1972.

ROMEO AND JULIET II
a poem by Peg Balfour

Balfour offers a different end to the romance had Romeo and Juliet not died. In this version they remained in Verona.

SUGGESTED STRATEGIES

Writing for Newspapers and Television: Assuming Romeo and Juliet do not die after the traumatic events, have groups of students write a follow-up news story ten years later titled "Where Are They Now?" Either videotape the newscasts or have one person from each group read the newscast to the class. Afterwards, the class could vote on which group provided the most believable story.

REVIEW QUESTIONS

1. What is the tone of this poem?
2. Compare the poems "Purgatory" and "Romeo and Juliet II." How are they similar? How are they different? Include in your answer not only content, but style, tone, rhythm, and images.

THE AUTHOR

Peg Balfour (1922–) lives in Kitchener, Ontario. She has won two Southwestern Library Awards for her poetry, and has self-published several books including a juvenile novel *A Tango of Leaves*.

OR ELSE FOR LOVE
a drama by Robert Nathan

As with the two poems on pages 168 and 169 in the student text, Juliet and Romeo have found more than they envisioned when pledging their love in a romantic orchard in Verona.

SUGGESTED STRATEGIES

Writing Poetry: Have the students write a poem based on the events as chronicled in this dramatic excerpt. Ask each of the students to write either from the point of view of Friar Laurence, Romeo, or Juliet (as a first-person narrator) or as an observer (a third-person narrator). When the students are satisfied with their poem, ask them to do an artistically arranged hand-written or computer-generated copy for displaying in the class.

Discussing Language: Ask three students to read the parts aloud to the class. Tell the students to listen carefully with their eyes closed to the playwright's use of language. Divide the class into groups and have them discuss their personal response to the language—whether or not they liked it, how it compared with Shakespeare's, the devices used (metaphors, alliteration, similes), and so on. Tell them to avoid reacting to the plot and concentrate on how the playwright used words to convey his ideas.

REVIEW QUESTIONS

1. How much time has passed?
2. What is the first deviation from the original play in this version?
3. How is the use of the nightingale and lark different from the original? How is it the same?
4. Why does this love story also end sadly?

THE AUTHOR

Robert Nathan (1894–1985) was a New York-born lecturer, novelist, screen writer, playwright, and poet. He is best known for his novels *The Bishop's Wife* and *Portrait of Jenny.*

Infusing Workforce Skills into the Teaching of Shakespeare:

New Ways to Look at the Curriculum

As students move into the 21st century, they will find that employment-related skills are increasingly important. Our students will be required to be

- active problem solvers
- cooperative workers and planners
- good oral and written communicators
- informed technology users
- systems planners
- information processors
- innovative managers and team leaders

At one time, these skills were needed by only a few of the employees within any company. Today, most workers need these strengths.

Many of the activities that are commonly done in the classroom can help students develop these skills. It's a question of maximizing opportunities to present information orally, problem solve, work in groups, write in a variety of formats, and synthesize information. The assignments in this Appendix are specifically designed to build the skills that will be needed in the workforce of the future.

Innovative Thinking (The Prologue)

Skills: This is a "let's get interested" assignment. It requires students to be innovative and creative while working cooperatively together. They will also use comprehension and analytic skills to process complex information and for problem solving.

Assignment: Divide the class into groups of four. Hand out copies of The Prologue and allow about five minutes for the students to read the text in order to get a "sense" of the lines. Give each group a sheet of white paper and several coloured markers or pencils. Ask the students to imagine the sonnet is a song and to work cooperatively to create a design for a CD insert based on the words to the "song." You might wish to have available several CDs so the students can see the various elements that are part of a CD insert design. Explain that in the music industry, several people would have input into creative work such as this.

Expressing Opinions (Act 1, Scene 1)

Skills: This assignment offers the students a chance to work cooperatively, analyze situations, and problem solve. They will get practice speaking in front of a group of people and will recognize that everyone's interpretation is different. This stresses that a problem often must be approached from several perspectives.

Assignment: Divide the students into groups of five. Ask each group to subdivide themselves and prepare to do a reading of lines 1–64. There are a total of five parts in this section. After the parts have been assigned, give the groups about ten minutes to prepare the reading. Then have each group perform their lines. Stress to the students that they should place their own interpretations on the words and to do their reading enthusiastically. Explain that their opinion on how the lines should be read is as valid as the next person's. They will also observe how others "solved the problem" of reading the lines. Encouraging readings of this sort will help prepare students for business situations that require speaking at meetings and addressing larger groups.

Writing Observations (Act 1, Scene 2)

Skills: One of the most important skills a student can learn is to write clearly and concisely. In this assignment, they will read, write, and synthesize information from research, literary readings, and their own personal life. They will be learning to extract relevant facts and draw conclusions about that information—valuable employment-related skills.

Assignment: Ask the students to pretend that they are a teenager in the Elizabethan era. They are to write about the events in this scene in their journal, perhaps in diary style, as if they were living at that time.

Tell the students they will get a sense of the setting and events from Lord Capulet and Paris's conversation, the servant's words, and the lines from Benvolio and Romeo's discussion. Have the students use this dialogue and books or articles about the period, such as *Shakespeare Alive!* by Joseph Papp, to write their impressions. Be sure to have the students refer to actual events from the play and historical facts.

Visual Presentations (Act 1, Scene 4)

Skills: Students are asked to log, identify, categorize, defend, and illustrate ideas. The business skills applications come from organizing facts and creating a visual representation to symbolize words. The taking of words and forming them into images is not only an artistic endeavour, but also a synthesizing and a finding of the true source of importance within a group of words, a concept, or a thought.

Assignment: Tell the students that this scene is full of "literary poetry"—figures of speech such as metaphors, similes, personification. After reading the scene, give them each a copy of Blackline Master 3 on p. 41. to record at least eight quotations that got their attention, the appeal of the quotations, and the type of literary device used. From their list ask the students to choose one that is particularly appealing and transfer it to a poster board in the form of a group of symbols. Remind them to be sure to include the quote on the poster, and that they shold be prepared to explain and defend their interpretation.

A Renaissance Feast (Act 1, Scene 5)

Skills: This assignment easily lends itself to workforce concepts. First, the students are divided into committees to solve problems. Second, they will be anticipating needs that they do not normally address. Third, they will be analyzing their own efforts. These are all essential skills for real-world group decision making. Fourth, they are performing research, a cornerstone of the innovative thinking needed in business today. Fifth, as a learning tool, they will perform an after-the-event analysis.

Assignment: Have your students create a Renaissance Feast. See also the "Feast and Dance" activity in Act 1, Scene 5 on page 12 of this Guide. Give the students a copy of Blackline Master 4 on p. 42 to help them develop their plans. Divide the students into four committees as outlined on the BLM. The students should research appropriate foods, decorations, entertainment, and typical furnishings. After the event, get together as a class and discuss what worked and what didn't, and what was learned from the experience (use the questions on the handout for this).

Working in Groups (Act 2, Prologue)

Skills: Students are asked to do an analysis of text in order to extract the most important information from a document. They are then asked to take that information and communicate it to an audience. They will be problem solving, working in teams, and speaking to a group.

Assignment: Shakespeare's uses dumb shows in some of his plays. Explain the term "dumb show" to the students if they do not already know it (or ask them to find out for themselves): It is a pantomime often used in Elizabethan drama to foreshadow for the audience upcoming action. Divide the students into groups and have them create a dumb show for this prologue. Explain the need for communicating the most important elements of the text so the audience can anticipate future events.

Few for the Many (Act 2, Scene 3)

Skills: Surveying opinions, decision making, analysis, and problem solving are the workforce skills used in this assignment. When a concept is moved from the curriculum to the real world, the learning becomes relative to the student. A businesslike report is also required for this assignment.

Assignment: Friar Lawrence agrees to the marriage of Romeo and Juliet for the noble purpose of bringing the enmity between the Capulets and the Montagues to an end. Have the students obtain an answer to the following question from five individuals (not fellow students): What instance can you think of in a local, national, or international situation, where a leader has decided to allow a certain action to occur in the hope that it will solve a much larger (perceived) problem? Have the students record the responses they receive and then make a statement of support or non-support, using the Friar's rationale as a comparison. Ask them to present their findings to the class as a computer-generated chart.

Scene Design (Act 3, Scene 1)

Skills: This activity has the students not only using higher order thinking, synthesis, team work, and oral communication, but it also asks them to integrate math and drafting skills into the English class. This integration of disciplines is a necessary skill in the workforce, as is presenting material in a professional manner.

Assignment: Though it is easy to imagine this scene's fight taking place on a neighbourhood street, it is more difficult to visualize and produce the same effects on a stage. Using drawings done to scale, have pairs of students create a stage set on which it is possible for this scene to take place. Multiple levels may enhance their designs.

The students will need to create a representation for each series of movements to make sure their set is viable. They will also need to provide stage directions that reflect their design. Display the projects in the class, and tell the students to be prepared to explain their design and answer questions about it.

Maslow's Hierarchy (Act 4, Scene 3 and Act 5, Scene 1)

Part 1—The Chart

Skills: This activity requires students to use business terminology, followed by the communication of that information in a visual display—a typical business concept.

Assignment: Distribute Maslow's Hierarchy of Personal Need to the students. (Blackline Master 5, p. 43). Go over it briefly with them. Then explain that they are to create a poster that illustrates where the actions and emotions of Juliet (Act 4, Scene 3) and Romeo (Act 5, Scene 1) fit on this chart. Encourage the students to use a professional, businesslike approach to their presentation. Suggest they imagine the poster will be used as a visual in a talk being given about the play *Romeo and Juliet* by a famous Shakespearean scholar. Display the posters in the class.

Part 2—Discussion

Skills: As the students discuss the issue of hierarchal need, they will be participating in a businesslike exchange of ideas. They will enounter arguments and other types of reasoning and be practising oral communication. Encourage interaction of thinking and reasoning as students discuss their opinions.

Assignment: Have the students divide into groups of four and discuss the levels of hierarchal need that are met and lacking in each of the characters. Explain that their group is a committee that is meeting to discuss a particular business issue and to act accordingly. Afterward, ask each group to prepare a business report on their findings and conclusions.

Visual Presentation (Act 5, Scene 1)

Skills: The students will research a product and then design a flier in a businesslike format to advertise that product. They will also use advertising techniques and computer technology.

Assignment: Herbs and potions play an important part in this play. Ask the students to research eight or more plants that have medicinal properties. You may prefer to divide the students into groups and assign two plants to each group for research. Then ask each group to design a computer-generated flier advertising their product (in the form of a living plant). For each plant, the student will need to provide the scientific name, the common name, a drawing, and its properties and uses. Remind the students the purpose of their flier: Without making extravagant or misleading claims about the plant, make sure it is attractive, creative, and informative.

Proposal (Final Assignment)

Skills: Proposals are common formats in business. Writing such a proposal is also an effective way for getting students to take a concept from literature and apply it to the real world. It will also ask them to address a current issue in society. The students will research real situations, as well as legal guidelines.

Assignment: Tell the students that because of the breadth and depth required for many proposals, they often are the work of more than one person. Distribute Blackline Master 6 on p. 44. Explain that the root problem in *Romeo and Juliet* is primarily prejudice. Divide the class into groups and ask them to work cooperatively to develop a legitimate means of solving a problem in society that has prejudice as its foundation. They may choose any situation as long as it has true significance. Ask them to present their proposal in the format outlined on the Proposal handout.

—— BLM 1 ——

Create your own Shakespearean sounding insults

The words in the following lists all come from Shakespeare's plays. To create your own Shakespearean sounding insults, choose a word from each of the columns and begin your invective with "Thou" or "You."

Column A	Column B	Column C
abhorred	accursed	acquaintance
bloody	abominable	canker-blossom
brawling	base	block
complete	brutish	clown
craven	calumnious	corruptor
currish	crafty	counterfeit
detestable	disloyal	coward
dishonest	dizzy-eyed	defiler
droning	doting	dwarf
dull	execrable	fiend
errant	fantastical	filth
false	gross	fishmonger
fawning	headstrong	fool
flattering	hollow-hearted	fustilarian
foolish	horrible	gossip
foul	hyperbolical	hellhound
gleeking	ill-breeding	hugger-mugger
goatish	impudent	jolthead
idle-pated	insolent	knave
impertinent	irksome	lewdster
infectious	jealous	louse
loathsome	joyless	lout
loggerheaded	leprous	lunatic
malignant	lily–livered	minimus
mewling	loathsomest	minion
mindless	lowborn	miscreant
naughty	madcap	monster
pestilent	mangy	moon-calf
petty	motley-minded	paraquito
puking	mumbling	peasant
puny	noise–maker	peacock
rank	notorious	quintessence
saucy	onion-eyed	rascal
scurvy	peevish	ratcatcher
shallow	plume-plucked	rioter
strange	pox-marked	rogue
surly	proud-minded	ruffian
tedious	putrified	sluggard
unseemly	rotten	swine
vain	rude	thing
villainous	rump-fed	traitor
waspish	scornful	varlot
wayward	unjust	vassal
worthless	untaught	villain
wretched	vile	worm

—— BLM 2 ——

(Act 1, Scene 4)

Cut the following quotes apart and distribute them randomly to your students. Give one quote to each of the nine groups. Follow the instructions given on page 11 of this Guide.

✂ ....

I see Queen Mab hath been with you

✂ ....

...she comes/In a shape no bigger than an agate stone

✂ ....

I dreamt a dream tonight

✂ ....

And in this state she gallops night by night/
Through lover's brains, and then they dream of love.

✂ ....

What curious eye doth quote deformities?

✂ ....

Her chariot is an empty hazelnut

✂ ....

You have dancing shoes
With nimble soles, I have a soul of lead

✂ ....

Thou talkest of nothing

✂ ....

True, I talk of dreams

✂ ....

Literary Devices
(Act 1, Scene 3)

The following literary devices are used frequently in literature, and Shakespeare's plays are a wealthy source of these word images. Record in your notebook as many as you can find from Act 1, Scene 3.

Literary Device	Literary Device
allusion: a brief reference to a person, event, or place, real or fictitious, or to a work of art.	To say: *"I am Lazarus, come from the dead,/ Come back to tell you all, I shall tell you all"* T. S. Elliott
alliteration: repetition of consonant sounds at the beginning of words.	*High harvest for the autumn's gathering* Dorothy Livesay
apostrophe: directly addressing an absent person, an abstract concept, or an inanimate object as if it were present and able to listen.	*O Shenandoah, I long to hear you,* Walt Whitman.
conceit: a very elaborate comparison of two very dissimilar things.	*I find no peace; and all my war is done; I fear and hope; I burn, and freeze in ice* Sir Thomas Wyatt
euphon: a combination of sounds that are pleasing to the ear.	*Silver honey dripping from the swarm of bees / Earth is a waxen cell of the world comb* Jean Toomer
simile: compares what is named using the words like, as, as if, as though.	*Christmas drew near, like the muzzle of a wolf.* Roch Carrier
metaphor: a word or phrase meaning one thing but used to describe something else.	*I too am a rare / Pattern.* Amy Lowell
onomatopoeia: a word whose pronun-ciation imitates or suggests its meaning.	*The moan of doves in immemorial elms, / And murmur of innumerable bees* Alfred Lord Tennyson.
personification: giving human characteristics to a non-human entity	*the valour glittered fiercely* Rita Joe

Once you have found examples of the above, increase your familiarity with these devices.

1. Find at least two examples for each device from the play as a whole.
2. Use pictures, drawings, or graphics to enhance your examples.
3. Find at least one other example for each from sources other than the play.
4. Create a poem in which you use five or more of the devices. (about 20 lines)
5. Keep these samples in your writing folder as a reminder to use literary devices to enhance your writing.

—— BLM 4 ——

A Renaissance Feast
(Act 1, Scene 5)

During Shakespeare's time it was not unusual for groups to plan a feast and then present a play as entertainment in conjunction with the feast. As part of our study of *Romeo and Juliet,* we will do the same.

1. There will be the following committees:
- entertainment
- food
- decorations
- seating/tables/furnishings

Everyone must serve on one of the above committees.
Everyone will be on clean-up duty.

2. Each committee will have a chairperson who will provide written reports to the teacher at specified times. These reports will include:
- committee decisions
- time line for actions
- assigned duties
- analysis of the group process

3. Each decision of the committee must be based on research regarding what the people of the 16th century probably would have done. Though it will be impossible to exactly duplicate food, entertainment, and decorations of the time, it should be as authentic as possible.

4. Groups will be graded on the following:
a. Participation
b. Success of the reenactment (authenticity)
c. Written narrative reflecting what was learned from the experience, including:
- What worked well?
- What did not work?
- Why were you unable to exactly replicate a particular activity or item?
- What would you do differently?
- What would you change?

—— BLM 5 ——

Maslow's Hierarchy of Personal Need (Act 4, Scene 3 and Act 5, Scene 1)

All people, in whatever stage of life, have basic needs. A psychologist named Abraham Maslow created a chart of these needs and the schedule of meeting them. All of us are able to move from the most basic physical need to the most intense psychological need by meeting one need and then reaching for the next level.

Physiological Needs
Housing
Food
Clothing ➡

Safety Needs
Freedom from Illness
Health Care as Needed
Safe Conditions ➡

Social Needs
Friends
Organizations
Love ➡

Self-Esteem Needs
Respect from Others
Respect for Self ➡

Self-Actualization Needs
True Understanding and
Acceptance of Self

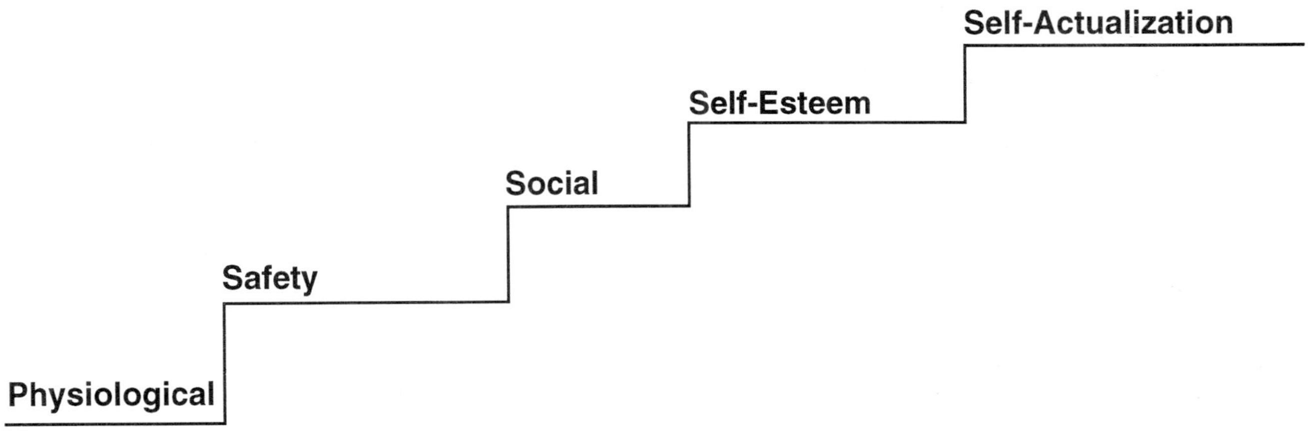

Think about Romeo and Juliet. Which of their needs are met in the play? How are these needs met? Who helps to meet them? What needs are not met? Who helps to prevent the need being met?

Create a poster that illustrates where the actions and emotions of Juliet (in Act 4, Scene 3) and Romeo (in Act 5, Scene 1) fit on the above chart.

Use a professional, businesslike approach. Imagine that your poster will be included as a visual in a talk about the play *Romeo and Juliet* by a famous Shakespearean scholar.

Proposal

Create a proposal that parellels some of the concepts about prejudice in the play *Romeo and Juliet,* along with any related source materials that are appropriate.

Choose a situation existing today that creates problems for society as a whole and that has a foundation in prejudice. Your situation may be local, national, or international. The only requirement is that it have true significance.

Explain the root of the problem and propose a means of solving it. Use the following guidelines to structure your proposal.

Proposal Directions

- Divide the written information into the following subheadings.

  [1] *Introduction* — Include
  a) the agent that propagates the prejudice,
  b) the history of its growth,
  c) its current standing,
  d) the way in which your sources offer parellel views of the problem.

  [2] *Needs Statement* — Explain why a solution is needed and the projected outcome of ignoring this issue. Cite sources for possible outcomes.

  [3] *Goals Statement* — Explain what the goal is, together with your purpose for addressing the issue. Use examples to show what the goal should be.

  [4] *Plan/Results Statement* — List your plans for solving the problem. Use examples to illustrate what might have been, had events been handled without prejudice.

  [5] *Conclusion* — Write a summation of what will be accomplished and prevented by following this proposal.

- Present your Proposal in a businesslike manner. Use a computer if possible and have visuals (pictures, graphics, charts) to support your information. Appearance is an important part of this assignment.

- Be sure to quote your sources carefully and provide an accurate list of those sources.

- Present your Proposal to the class.

—— **BLM 7** ——

Romeo and Juliet
Mythology Vocabulary

Listed below are some of the allusions from the play that you might not know. Define five of the references below by explaining the situation for which the character is associated.

1. Aurora ______________________

2. Cupid ______________________

3. Dian ______________________

4. Tartar ______________________

5. Venus ______________________

6. Cynthia ______________________

7. Dido ______________________

8. Helen ______________________

9. Hero ______________________

10. Thisbe ______________________

Using a large sheet of paper or poster board, create a mural that depicts some of the references listed and defined above. For this mural there should be a connecting theme among all of the elements on the mural. Remember to package your project in a very visual and creative manner.

Reading the First Folio
Romeo and Juliet

The spoken and written English of the time of Shakespeare is not the exact same English that is used today. At that time, the language was being clearly defined for the first time. The first real dictionary of the English language was written by Samuel Johnson nearly 150 years after Shakespeare wrote his plays.

Because of this, there were no real standards of spelling and punctuation. Typesetters had to set the words for books one letter at a time. If a section of the book contained too many **u**'s, then the compositor might switch to **v**'s. No one was concerned with the lack of standards because no rules had really been established. In a First Folio edition, the letters **u**, **i**, **v**, and **j** might be used interchangeably. Sometimes a **v**, **w** or **vv** might be also used interchangeably. There were two types of **s**'s. One was called a tall s and looked like ſ . You will notice that this tall s looks like an f. The other was a regular **s**.

In your group, as you read through the sample First Folio page found on page 7 of your text, remember the interchangeable letters and two different s's. If you read the text out loud, you will be able to hear what certain words should be. Don't be surprised if you confuse words like **wiſdom**. It looks like wisdom, but it is actually wifedom. Remember the spelling will not be consistent, nor will the words be ones you find familiar. The average person's vocabulary is about 7000 words; Shakespeare's vocabulary was 3 times that. Also consider that language evolves. A word that was used in the 1600s may not be as common today.

You and your group members are to translate the Prince's speech that appears at the bottom of the right side of page 7 in your text. Write each line in modern spelling, but don't change the wording.

Good luck!

—— BLM 9 ——

Idea Starters
Romeo and Juliet

Essay Questions

Answer one of the following in essay format. Be sure to use an introduction that contains a thesis statement, specific examples from the play for support to support your topics, and a concluding statement. Remember to adhere to the rules of good composition.

or

Journal Writing

Respond to one of the following as a journal entry. As you write, think of the play text, other literary selections you have read, songs, or real life.

1. Romeo's impulsiveness is one possible cause for the deaths of the two young people. Prove that it was not his impulsiveness but some other factor that caused the deaths.
2. What kind of person is the character of Tybalt? Identify at least three personality traits and prove that they exist from words and actions that are found within the play.
3. Jeanne Roberts says "Shakespeare's evolution in depicting male control of Nature and women seems to parallel what was actually happening in seventeenth-century society." What is your reaction to this quotation? Do you feel that this is true?
4. Using quotes from the play, describe the kind of love that Romeo and Juliet had for each other.
5. Juliet was in reality very innocent. She had never been in love before she saw Romeo. She married him quickly. Neither she nor Romeo really took time to think; they just reacted. After Romeo kills Tybalt, everyone that Juliet loves or depends upon, for one reason or another, abandons her. This abandonment causes her death. Either prove or disprove this statement using examples from the text.
6. Some critics say that Mercutio's Queen Mab speech is the summation of the real theme of the play. Prove this statement by using examples from the text.
7. Use three quotations from the text that you feel establish the concept of "star-crossed lovers" in a theme that discusses the inevitability of the outcome of Romeo and Juliet.
8. Choose one of the related readings that has been provided to you. Consider the mirror image of the play that this work creates. How does it change or reinforce your feelings about occurrences in the play? Write an essay that reveals its impact.
9. Choose one of the following quotes and discuss who said it, why it was said, and the importance of what the quote means.
   "Oh, I am Fortune's fool."
   "A word and a blow."
   "Good night, good night! parting is such sweet sorrow."
   "Past hope, past care, past help!"
   "See what a scourge is laid upon your hate."
   "Tis the nightingale..."
   "Here's much to do with hate, but more with love"
   "You kiss by the book."
   "O serpent heart, hid with a flowering face!"
   "Then window, let day in, and let life out."
   "O swear not by the moon, the inconstant moon"
   "Then I defy you, stars"
   "And death's pale flag is not advanced there"
   "What's in a name? That which we call a rose"
   "He jests at scars that never felt a wound"
10. One motivator in the actions of the characters could be chance. Think of the instances in the play where something occurs that just happens to cause something to go wrong or someone to make a poor decision. The excelleration of actions by certain characters maximizes this effect. In an essay discuss the impact of chance on the characters of the play.

RESOURCE SHELF

Teacher Resources

CPB Teachers' Digest, CCI/Crosby Publishing, 141 Portland Street, Suite 7100, Cambridge, MA 02139. This magazine provides sources and ideas for teachers.

O'Brien, Peggy, editor, *Shakespeare Set Free.* New York: Washington Square Press, 1993.

Shakespeare, Georgetown University, P. O. Box 571006, Washington D. C. 20057.
An inexpensive teacher resource magazine for ideas about teaching Shakespeare.

Web sites

The Folger Shakespeare Library: http://www.folger.edu/menu.htm
This site was partially finished as of January 1997; it will provide valuable sources for teachers and researchers once it is finished.

Library of Congress: http://cweb.loc.gov/
This website offers access to the Library of Congress catalogue. The Library of Congress is working in collaboration with some of the major universities in the nation to create digital access to documents.

Internet Movie Database: http://us.imdb.com/
This source provides the names, casts, and reviews for most movies. This site is an excellent tool for finding films suitable for use in the classroom.

Serious Links: http://www.wsu.edu:8080/~brians/favorite_sites.html
This site, created by Paul Brians from Washington State University, is a user-friendly access to many Web sites. It is indexed in categories that meet the needs of teachers looking for research information or useful websites.

Films and Videos Based on Romeo and Juliet

Romeo and Juliet (1936). Directed by George Cukor with a strong cast, including John Barrymore. An early black and white version of the play.

West Side Story (1961). Directed by Jerome Robbins and Robert Wise. A musical version of *Romeo and Juliet* set in New York. A strong cast and script.

Romeo and Juliet (1968). Directed by Frano Zeffirelli. A strong cast done in traditional Shakespearean style.

William Shakespeare's Romeo and Juliet (1996). Directed by Baz Luhrmann. Romeo and Juliet are transported to the gangs of Verona Beach, California. A strong cast in a very stylized, nontraditional version of the play. A vibrant version for those with receptive minds.

More Related Readings

Alberti, Rafael. "Romeo and Juliet." Translated from the Spanish by Alan Sillitoe from *An Anthology of Poetry for Shakespeare.* Selected by Charles Osborne. Southwark: Bishopsgate Press, 1988.

Cavendish, Margaret. *The Convent of Pleasure.* A text written by a woman about the day-to-day life of women during the Renaissance.

Chavez, Fray Angelico. "A Romeo and Juliet Story in Early New Mexico," from *The Short Stories of Fray Angelico Chavez.* Albuquerque: University of New Mexico Press, 1987.

Clark, Mary Cowden. "Juliet: The White Dove of Verona," from *The Girlhood of Shakespeare's Heroines, Volume II.* London: J. M. Dent.

Corlis, Richard. Review of the movie *Romeo and Juliet* in *Time Magazine,* November 4, 1996.

Dennis, C. J. "The Play," in *The Sentimental Bloke and Other Verses.* Syndey: Angus and Robertson, 1950.

Epstein, Norrie. "Romeo and Juliet" in *The Friendly Shakespeare.* New York. Viking. 1993.

Holmer, Joan O. "Draw If You Be Men, Saviolo's Significance for Romeo and Juliet" in *Shakespeare Quarterly.* 45, Summer, 1994

Loedhas, Sorche Nic. "The Gay Goss-Hawk from Heather and Broom" from *Tales of the Scottish Highlands.* New York: Holt, Rinehart and Winston.

Miles, Josephine. "Maxim." from *Cries of the Spirit, A Celebration of Women's Spirituality.* Edited by Marilyn Sewell. Boston: Beacon Press, 1991

Papp, Joseph and Elizabeth Kirkland. *Shakespeare Alive!* New York: Bantam Books, 1988.

Pearce, Craig and Luhrmann, Baz. *William Shakespeare's Romeo and Juliet: The Contemporary Film from The Classic Play.* Laurel-Leaf Books, 1996

Schimel, Lawrence. "Swear Not by the Moon" from *Weird Tales from Shakespeare.* Edited by Katherine Kerry and Martin H. Greenberg. New York: Daw Books, Inc., 1994.

Warmbrod, Nancy Compton "A Psychological Profile of Shakespeare's Juliet: or Was It Merely Hormones?" *English Journal.* December, 1980.